SHEPHERD AND SERVANT

The Spiritual Legacy of Saint Dunstan

Douglas Dales

SLG Press
Convent of the Incarnation
Fairacres Oxford

ISBN 0 7283 01547
ISSN 0307-1405

Printed by Will Print, Oxford, England

Introduction

ST DUNSTAN was regarded as the most outstanding of the English saints in the years leading up to the Norman Conquest. The fact that he is not still venerated as a patron saint of England is due to the deliberate action of the Normans in suppressing his memory at Canterbury for a generation. Although St Anselm restored Dunstan's cult, the murder of Thomas Becket and his subsequent commemoration eclipsed the fundamental importance of Dunstan in English church history.

When the Reformation destroyed the monasteries, Dunstan's oblivion was almost complete, and only unfavourable legends persisted, portraying him as an obscurantist monk. Gradually in the twentieth century, historians have recovered his memory, and it was in 1988, the millennium of his death, that the site of his burial-place was marked again, to the right of the high altar in Canterbury Cathedral. In the same year, the place of his birth was also commemorated at Baltonsborough, near Glastonbury in Somerset. In 1991, a monk of the Pechersk Lavra in Kiev, the mother house of Russian monasticism, drew an icon of St Dunstan as a symbol of reconciliation and hope between east and west; it now hangs in the chapel of the Abbey House in Glastonbury.

Yet by any standards, the life and achievements of Dunstan must rank as notable and formative in the long history of English Christianity. He was born around the year 909, and died just after Ascension in 988. The first part of his life was associated with Glastonbury where he was educated, and where in the years after 942 he established Benedictine monastic life. In 960 he was made Archbishop of Canterbury, and for 28 years he presided over far-reaching developments and reforms in English church and society. He was regarded

1

as a saint in his own lifetime, and his tomb at Canterbury became a place of pilgrimage and miracles.

Dunstan left little in writing, and evidence of his intellectual and artistic gifts can only be detected fragmentarily in the manuscripts that remain. Yet the shape and development of church and society in England in the tenth century only really begin to make sense in the light of his career and influence. He embodied and articulated many of the most fundamental values and beliefs of the Anglo-Saxon church as it had developed over four hundred years since the coming of St Augustine from Rome to Canterbury. He was profoundly devoted to the memory and teaching of St Gregory the Great, whom he and his church regarded as the 'Apostle of the English'. His spiritual stature can only now be measured, however, by the shape and character of the church and society that grew under his leadership and guidance.

His spirituality and its impact can, on the other hand, be discerned indirectly but deeply. There are several places to look, and these are rich and interesting sources, which serve as mirrors catching the spiritual light he shed forth.

Firstly, there is the famous picture commissioned and completed by Dunstan himself while he was Abbot of Glastonbury, included in one of the books he edited there. Then there is the prologue he drafted to the *Regularis Concordia*, drawn up at Winchester in 970 to regulate the newly reformed and restored Benedictine monasteries for men and women in England. There is the political theology implicit in the Coronation Order which Dunstan developed in 973, and which still underlies the present rite. There are also the first two *Lives* of the saint, written within fifteen years of his death, for those who knew him well at Canterbury. Finally there is liturgical material, some of which was directly associated with him, by which his memory and cult were commemorated at Canterbury Cathedral and elsewhere.

The Vision of a Monk

The first biographer of Dunstan describes the saint as a devoted scholar, gifted artist and musician. His scholarly interest may be detected in his handwritten corrections found in several manuscripts known to have been at Glastonbury during his time as abbot. In one of these, now in the Bodleian library in Oxford, there is a remarkable line drawing of himself as a monk, kneeling at the feet of Christ. In many ways this is the most moving and powerful icon of the spiritual vision that inspired his life and work.

Christ is portrayed as the Wisdom of God, a monumental and majestic figure, drawn in flowing outlines and adorned with a reddened halo. It is a figure similar to several others known to have emerged from Dunstan's circle later at Canterbury, and Christ's posture is comparable to contemporary pictures of the Transfiguration. He looks away from the tiny figure of the praying monk who, as the disciples on Mount Tabor, lies prostrate on the ground. It is quite possible that Dunstan was portraying a vision that he had experienced of Christ in heavenly glory. The first *Life* recounts several such episodes throughout his spiritual life.

The picture appears to show this vision occurring on a hill that may well depict the Tor at Glastonbury, which was a place of prayer and eremitic life at that time. Certainly Dunstan himself was formed as a young priest in such a contemplative tradition, which owed much to long-standing Irish influences at Glastonbury.

Dunstan portrays himself as a monk, with his cowl thrown half back. In this he emulates a similar picture that he may have seen from the Continent. This was drawn by the great Benedictine scholar Hrabanus Maur, who lived in France in the ninth century, of himself kneeling at the foot of the Cross. The revival of monasticism which Dunstan helped to initiate in England owed much to similar developments in

Europe in the ninth and tenth centuries; and when he was exiled in 956 for political reasons, Dunstan fled for a while to a reformed Benedictine monastery at Ghent, in Flanders. The figure of Christ holds an inscribed book or tablet, on which are written words from the psalms: *Come, my children, and listen to me; and I will teach you the fear of the Lord. (Ps.34.11)* These words also occur in the preface to the Rule of St Benedict. The earliest biographer describes how Dunstan created the first Benedictine enclosure at Glastonbury and ruled over it directly as abbot for nearly sixteen years. In due time, many of the bishops as well as the abbots of the new monasteries were drawn from Glastonbury, having been his disciples. All the archbishops of Canterbury for the next hundred years came from this one monastic community.

Christ also holds a budding rod, symbolising the authority of God. Along it are inscribed further words from the psalms: *The rod of thy kingdom is the rod of righteousness. (Ps.45.6)* Christ is therefore portrayed as Teacher and also as Judge. Dunstan was himself highly regarded as a teacher of the young, well versed in law as well as theology. There remains a book of canon law that he corrected while Abbot of Glastonbury. Several charters also remain which were drafted there, and those who emerged to lead the English church as abbots and bishops were trained to be directly involved in the administration of justice. As Archbishop of Canterbury, Dunstan was active as the supreme judicial authority in the land after the king himself, for example setting aside papal dispensations from marriage which had been corruptly obtained in Rome. His influence may be detected in the moral tone of some of the laws that remain from Edgar's reign.

Dunstan enhanced the picture further by the discreet but effective introduction of colour. The highlighting of powerful line drawings in this way became a hall-mark of other manuscripts produced at Canterbury during his time there as archbishop. Such a figure could also serve as an outline for a

three-dimensional relief in stone or metal, or as a design for embroidered vestments. Dunstan was renowned as a skilled designer and metalworker throughout his life, and this drawing may have been a preliminary sketch for such a work of religious art.

Finally, this drawing incorporates a moving personal autograph that is very rare in the early middle ages. Above the head of the kneeling picture of himself, Dunstan has added a little prayer in his own handwriting: *I, Dunstan, beg the merciful Christ to protect me, lest the storms of the underworld swallow me up.* In the first *Life* of the saint, there are numerous stories told of how Dunstan had to endure great spiritual affliction from evil, trying to prevent him from creating at Glastonbury a strong centre of Christian education and religious life.

His life and career were beset by storms, human and spiritual. Opposition almost drove him abroad before being appointed to be Abbot of Glastonbury around the year 940, and fifteen years later he had to flee for his life into exile. Dunstan's spiritual achievement was not won without great conflict and cost to himself. But he was remembered by those who knew him, and in later folklore, as one who had withstood evil. This picture reflects that experience, and so opens a window into his spiritual life and teaching.

Spiritual Parents

Who laid the foundations for such a vocation and ministry? The person who wrote the first *Life* of Dunstan was clearly familiar with traditions surrounding the period of his life spent at Glastonbury, many of which may well have been Dunstan's own reminiscences. He indicates how the parents of Dunstan were a decisive influence upon his early sense of spiritual vocation. As a child, his father Heorstan took him, on one of many occasions, by boat to the Old Church in Glastonbury. That night while he was sleeping there,

Dunstan had a vision of 'an old man in snow-white robes' who intimated to him his future work in restoring monastic life there. Was this figure St Benedict, or perhaps St Cuthbert, who, it was believed, had appeared to Alfred the Great on the eve of his decisive battle against the Vikings at Edington in 878? Hindsight may well have laid the basis for later hagiographical embellishment; but this should not obscure a moment of genuine spiritual encounter between a child and God, through a vision of a saint.

Later in his life Dunstan had a vision of his mother Cynethrith in heaven, representing the Church as the Bride of Christ. The second *Life* also confirms her importance with a charming story of how, before Dunstan's birth, she sensed that the child still in her womb would be in some way remarkable. She and her husband were keeping Candlemas in the Old Church of Glastonbury when a sudden gust blew out all the candles. Hers was miraculously rekindled, and so light was spread throughout the church. Glastonbury was an ancient and holy shrine of the Mother of God, at which she sometimes appeared, and Dunstan always held St Mary in the highest veneration. Both these stories intimate the abiding influence of a mother upon her son as a mirror of the church, and of Mary who is the mother of the church, even though they are also stories typical of hagiography from this period.

No less important were those who proved to be his spiritual parents. His uncle Athelm, first Bishop of Wells and later Archbishop of Canterbury, introduced Dunstan to the court of King Athelstan. Later on there was another kinsman, Alphege 'the Bald', Bishop of Winchester. He was a person who had travelled to the Continent and had witnessed the revival of monastic life there. Alphege had taken private monastic vows, and he kept in touch with Dunstan, inviting him for a time to Winchester to serve as his chaplain, and persuading him to consider becoming a monk. This Dunstan at first refused to do, declaring that his intention was to marry his girlfriend rather than to put on the sheepskins of a monk! The bishop's prayer, and Dunstan's sharp illness, finally brought about a change of heart. But his reaction suggests that it was hard at that time to persuade intelligent young men to consider a vocation to the monastic life.

Communal religious life in England was, however, maintained among noble women in the early tenth century, quite a number of whom adopted a semi-eremitic way of life. To one of these women, Dunstan owed a very great deal. Ethelfleda was a member of the royal family who lived a semi-reclusive life near the Old Church at Glastonbury. She nurtured his spiritual life, and after her death left him the considerable landed wealth she possessed. He later used much of this bequest to endow the monasteries he restored and reformed. She was truly his spiritual mother, being a person of a deeply contemplative life, to whom, he believed, the Holy Spirit had appeared in resplendent light. Dunstan witnessed this moment as she was dying, and ministered to her spiritual needs to the end; she died shortly after receiving the Eucharist at his hand.

Dunstan's appointment to be Abbot of Glastonbury, around the year 942, was almost prevented by intrigue at court, and there were clearly many, clergy and nobility, who regarded him as a threat. The plan to revive Glastonbury as a Benedictine monastery would ultimately challenge the rights of those who held lands originally given to serve its religious community. Dunstan might well have gone abroad to Germany, where other English Christians were playing an active part in the revival of monastic life. However, the new young king, Edmund, after a narrow escape while hunting above Cheddar Gorge, had a change of heart, and hurried home to escort Dunstan to the ancient shrine of Glastonbury, charging him to create within it a genuine Benedictine monastery. This was in fulfilment of the policy pursued by his predecessor, King Athelstan, and other bishops and laity sympathetic to the revival of monastic life in England.

His appointment proved a turning point in the history of the English church, as well as in Dunstan's own life. For the next sixteen years or so, he persevered while Glastonbury became the seedbed for a steady growth of monastic renewal and reform across England. But he could not have progressed without the steadfast support of several bishops, led by Oda the Archbishop of Canterbury. Oda was of Viking origin and had personal contact with the monastery at Fleury, which claimed custody of the body of St Benedict. He sent there his own nephew, Oswald, later to become a close friend of Dunstan, who made him Bishop of Worcester, and Archbishop of York. In many ways Oda laid the foundations for Dunstan's later work as Archbishop of Canterbury by his reforms in the church, and after his death Dunstan venerated his tomb every time he passed it with the words, 'here lies Oda the Good.'

A picture emerges of the range of Dunstan's spiritual and theological reading from the books that bear evidence of his scholarly corrections. This was the tradition that nurtured his spiritual formation. These include an exposition of the Rule of St Benedict by Smaragdus, a copy of St Augustine's *Enchiridion*, and a commentary by Primasius on the Apocalypse, as well as one by Caesarius of Arles. Dunstan's interest in poetry is reflected in his annotations of a copy of Aldhelm's *Carmen de Virginitate*, and in a copy he commissioned of Boethius' *De Consolatione Philosophiae*. The book in which his famous drawing of Christ is inserted comprises many diverse areas of interest, poetical, theological and liturgical, and his corrections to a copy of Bede's *De Temporum Ratione* reflect his practical interests as a churchman in the calculation of sacred time. As Abbot of Glastonbury, and later as Archbishop of Canterbury, he drew upon these resources as an active reformer and spiritual teacher of the church.

The Advice of an Abbot

Glastonbury prospered under Dunstan's leadership, and in the early 950s Ethelwold, a friend and contemporary of Dunstan, who had been his disciple at Glastonbury, founded with the support of the royal family a second Benedictine monastery at Abingdon. After Dunstan was made Archbishop of Canterbury in 960, he appointed Ethelwold to Winchester and Oswald to Worcester to spearhead the systematic revival of monastic life throughout England. Ethelwold founded monasteries in the Old and New Minsters at Winchester, and he also reformed the royal Nunnaminster there. He went on to renew monasteries on the ancient sites of Ely and Peterborough, while Oswald gradually converted the cathedral at Worcester into a monastic community, and created the new foundation of Ramsey in the East Anglian fens. Dunstan himself slowly converted the cathedral community at Canterbury into a monastic one, and helped reform the ancient monastery of St Augustine's there. He also took a personal interest in reforming the old royal monasteries of Malmesbury and Westminster, as well as continuing to supervise his own community at Glastonbury. By the time of Dunstan's death in 988, over two dozen monasteries had been created, reformed or revived, most of which survived until the Reformation.

A clear policy lay behind this movement, as is revealed in the decisions of a synod at Winchester in 963. The English reformers maintained lively links with their counterparts on the Continent, and the extent of this collaboration becomes clear in the *Regularis Concordia*, which was drawn up at another synod in Winchester in 973. This remarkable document is really a national act of uniformity to ensure the consistent observance of the Rule of St Benedict, drawing together the experience of the reformers on the continent, especially at Ghent and Fleury, and combining monastic life with the established customs of the English church. The distinct feature of the *Regularis Concordia* is the prominence given to prayers for the royal family, and the reliance placed by the monks on royal patronage.

Ethelwold probably drafted the document, but the political authority behind this unique statement was certainly Dunstan's as Archbishop of Canterbury. He was the diplomatic link with the papacy, whose permission he had sought in the beginning for this enterprise. He would also have had to carry with him the support of significant parts of the lay aristocracy, whose wealth actually secured the success and protection of individual monastic foundations. The prologue to the *Regularis Concordia* affords another window into the spiritual influence of St Dunstan.

This prologue reveals a clear understanding of Christian kingship, and a vision of the past that owed much to Bede's *Ecclesiastical History*. This work had actually been translated into English by command of Alfred the Great, and the picture painted by Bede inspired the monastic revival that he tried to initiate, but which only reached its fullness during Dunstan's primacy. Glastonbury and Canterbury became repositories of many relics of Northumbrian saints, as the kings of Wessex asserted their authority in the north of England against the Vikings. Alfred and his successors persistently claimed to be defenders of the Christian culture and tradition of all the English people, and Bede's *History* was central to their belief that they were recreating a lost 'golden age' of royal monasticism. The most striking symbol of this ideology was the devotion shown by the royal house of Wessex to the cult of St Cuthbert, whose uncorrupted body was adorned by their gifts, which may still be seen in the treasury at Durham Cathedral.

The cutting edge of Dunstan's reform, embodied in the *Regularis Concordia*, struck against the interests of the married clergy, who passed on church endowments and lands to their families by inheritance. This tendency, it was believed, had undermined monastic life in the past. It had also damaged the defensive strength of the earlier English kingdoms, because the lay owners and administrators of such 'church land' were immune from military service, and were thus able to evade taxes and other obligations. Bede himself had criticised this tendency more than two hundred years earlier.

Ethelwold was obliged to resort to forcible eviction to achieve his reforms at Winchester, and Dunstan had to battle against a sustained rearguard action by those whom his reform had dispossessed. Not all clergy were enamoured of monasticism, and Dunstan was forced to justify his reliance on the political support of the king. He did so in this prologue by depicting the king as acting on behalf of Christ, the Good Shepherd, and the queen as representing the Mother of God caring for the welfare of the church. In the end, the *Regularis Concordia* greatly enhanced the prestige of the monarchy, turning the monasteries into spiritual fortresses answerable in part to the king as well as to the church.

The main purpose of this agreement was, however, to secure unity among the new monasteries as to how they would observe the Rule of St Benedict in the spiritual interests of the English people and their ruler. The *Regularis Concordia* is an elaborate framework in which was set the essentially simple pattern laid down by St Benedict. In it Dunstan achieves a balance between enthusiasm, consensus and obedience, which is striking, and probably characteristic of his rule as Archbishop of Canterbury.

In this development of Benedictine monasticism, England and the Continental church marched in step. Dunstan himself spent about eighteen months in exile at the reformed monastery of St Peter's in Ghent. He maintained links of friendship there throughout his time at Canterbury, and it was from there that a monk wrote the second *Life* of Dunstan for the community at Canterbury Cathedral. Ethelwold and Oswald had their own direct links with Fleury, the heart of the Benedictine reform movement; Oswald lived there for some time at the behest of his uncle, Archbishop Oda.

The prologue pays tribute to the presence of monks from both communities as advisers to the English church in the formulation of this monastic agreement. Dunstan justified this policy by appeal to the instruction of St Gregory the Great to St Augustine, recorded by Bede, about the wisdom of drawing together all that was best in the church life he had encountered. Tribute is also paid in the prologue to the *Regularis Concordia* to the 'great and subtle judgement of reason' shown by Dunstan at this point for his skill in welding together traditional English customs with the experience of the Continental reformers.

One of the manuscripts remaining of the *Regularis Concordia* opens with a remarkable picture portraying King Edgar, flanked on either side by Dunstan and Ethelwold, with the actual text of the book flowing between them. Underneath the text a Benedictine monk supports the whole enterprise by his prayers and obedience. But the last part of the prologue seems to have been directly steered by Dunstan himself: 'Now in order to confirm the deliberations of the synod, Dunstan, the noble archbishop of our land, moved by a spirit of prophecy, providently and wisely added these further instructions'. These probably reflect his own personal convictions, and certain sensitive political concerns.

The first of these concerns is to protect the integrity of the royal nunneries, whose inmates were vulnerable to predatory princes and nobility, King Edgar himself being a notorious offender, even chasing his own cousins! Dunstan's second concern was that the recitation of the divine office should be sincere and dignified, and never perfunctory. He believed that intercession lay at the heart of monastic life and was the justification for its endowment and protection in national life. He then moves on to prescribe how abbots and abbesses are to be appointed: with royal approval, but as directed by the Rule of St Benedict. He also sets out the novel policy of creating bishops who are monks to rule over monastic cathedral communities; this was already the case at Winchester and Worcester, and gradually became so at Canterbury and elsewhere.

Dunstan tackles directly the vexed issue of how monastic lands could so easily revert to lay ownership and control. To avert this was the goal of the reformers and in the end they prevailed in large measure. Then he deals with more intimate matters affecting the good order of monastic life. He tells monks always to recite their offices, even on journeys, a practice, we are told in the first *Life*, that he always observed himself. He also emphasises that schoolboys in the care of monasteries need particular protection from corrupt monks. The boys at Canterbury remembered him gratefully after his death for his own care of them in this regard. Finally Dunstan is adamant about the need to secure the integrity of monastic enclosure, and to prevent abbots and abbesses from socialising with their landed kinsfolk. In all this he was obviously drawing on his own experience as Abbot of Glastonbury.

The Spirit of St Benedict

The Prologue closes with a fine statement of Benedictine intent:

> By the grace of our Lord Jesus Christ, we intend to maintain with all our power everything which has been handed down to us from our father Benedict, and which we have freely assumed for ourselves; measured amounts of food, clothing, fasting, ascetic discipline, and the virtue of obedience.

14

In fulfilment of our covenant, and with the utmost care as far as we are able, and led by the prompting of the Holy Spirit, we shall now set forth clearly in writing all those customs surrounding the holy Rule, as they have been observed everywhere by the holy disciples of Benedict himself, after much careful reflection and experience.

We seek only to establish brotherly unity, with the advice of our king, and trusting in the commandments of those who have gone before us in this way of life. We pray that all who observe these monastic customs in a spirit of peace and gratitude may receive eternal life as a reward from Him who makes men to be of one mind in a house, where God is the true King, even the Son of God, born of the holy Virgin, Who with the Father and the Holy Spirit lives and reigns forever. Amen.

The writer of the first *Life* of St Dunstan saw important parallels between him and St Benedict, the father of monks, and there are many details of his story that echo St Gregory the Great's *Life of St Benedict*. These also corroborate the main spiritual emphases of the *Regularis Concordia*. Perhaps the most central is Dunstan's devotion to the Eucharist and his insistence in the *Regularis Concordia* upon daily communion. Another important focus is upon the Cross:

> Lord Jesus Christ, I adore you ascending the Cross: may your Cross free me from all assaults of evil.
> Lord Jesus Christ, I adore you wounded on the cross: may your wounds heal my soul.
> Lord Jesus Christ, I adore you laid in the grave: may your death bring me life.
> Lord Jesus Christ, I adore you descending into hell to liberate its captives: I beg you never to let me enter there.
> Lord Jesus Christ, I adore your resurrection and ascension: have mercy upon me.
> Lord Jesus Christ, I adore your coming in judgement: when you come, do not enter into judgement with me, a sinner; but come rather to forgive than to condemn me.

The prayers included in the *Regularis Concordia* are an important memorial to the monastic spirituality which Dunstan did so much to nurture and develop. Many of them were traditional within English Christianity; for example the 'collect for purity' that opens the Anglican Eucharist is found already in use in Dunstan's time. Another prayer links devotion to the Eucharist and to the Cross:

Almighty God, Lord Jesus Christ, you stretched out your pure hands on the Cross for us, and redeemed us with your holy and precious blood; enable me so to feel and understand this mystery, that I may attain true repentance and unfailing perseverance all the days of my life.

Many of the earliest stories about Dunstan reveal the close bonds he enjoyed with members of his community at Glastonbury. There is no doubt that he was able to kindle great loyalty and spiritual fervour in those who came under his influence. This prayer captures the ethos of such a Benedictine community:

O God, you have poured out your gifts of love into the hearts of your faithful servants by the grace of your Holy Spirit: give them, we pray, of your mercy, health of body and soul, that they may love you with all their strength, and by that love do only those things that are pleasing to you. May they bear themselves with such humility and discretion in your holy service, that their worship may always delight you. We ask this through Jesus Christ our Lord.

The first *Life* of Dunstan paints this picture of him at the height of his powers:

Whenever he fulfilled the divine office in worship of Christ the Lord, and especially at celebrations of the Eucharist, Dunstan intoned with such integrity and devotion of mind that he seemed to be talking with the Lord Himself face to face, as if not at all irritated by the upheavals and quarrels of the people with whom he had been dealing moments before. Just like St Martin of Tours before him, Dunstan used simply to lift his eyes and hands to heaven, never relaxing from the spirit of prayer. At ordinations, or consecrations of churches or altars, or whenever he celebrated, he always shed copious tears in streams, which the Holy Spirit who ever dwelt within him drew forth mightily from his eyes.

Shepherd and Servant

Although Dunstan was a professed monk, his role as Abbot of Glastonbury and then Archbishop of Canterbury entailed a close involvement in politics. Like St Gregory the Great before him, his was no peaceful and secluded monastic vocation, even though he was a profoundly contemplative person. Indeed the first two *Lives* are indirectly commentaries on his changing relationships with several kings of Wessex. He was probably connected by kinship with King Athelstan. Certainly it was under that king, who reigned from 924 until 939, that Dunstan first appeared at court, and that the policy to reform Glastonbury was probably laid down. Eadred, who was a close personal friend of Dunstan, soon succeeded his nephew the young King Edmund, who had appointed Dunstan Abbot of Glastonbury in 942. It was during Eadred's reign that Ethelwold founded the monastery at Abingdon. On Eadred's death in 955 there was a reversal in Dunstan's fortunes and those of his aristocratic supporters, and he had to flee the kingdom, having openly challenged the new teenage king, Edwy, for his flagrant sexual immorality. Dunstan fled to Ghent in Flanders, narrowly escaping being killed, and lived there for a while, until circumstances changed and he was recalled by Edwy's brother, Edgar, to hold temporarily the sees of Worcester and London, before becoming Archbishop of Canterbury in 960.

This king had been a pupil of Dunstan and Ethelwold, and, although wayward in his personal life, Edgar proved amenable to the great programme of monastic renewal. His premature death in 975 provoked a succession crisis in which Dunstan intervened to secure the throne for Edgar's first son, Edward. He was, however, murdered by the supporters of his half-brother, Ethelred, who became king in 978. Relationships between the new king and his archbishop alternated between cool and stormy. Dunstan died in 988.

As Archbishop of Canterbury, Dunstan was closely involved in legislation, and the laws established in Edgar's reign became normative for all later Anglo-Saxon law. There was no separation made between church and secular law, and the church lent its authority to enforcing the law in an attempt to curb theft and violence. Sound currency, weights and measures were also of concern, and during Dunstan's time these were standardised and enforced. From the church's point of view, corruption of these directly afflicted the poor.

There were also laws that protected the autonomy and interests of the king's Danish and British subjects. Danelaw, the area inhabited in the north and east of the country by the Viking invaders, was the target of Christian mission throughout the tenth century as the church sought to re-establish its presence there. Before the century ended, missionaries went also from England to Scandinavia. During Dunstan's time, a close working partnership was established with the British churches in Cornwall and south Wales. So this policy of creating a secure and united kingdom rested on clear Christian principles, as well as on political and military considerations.

The clearest statement of Dunstan's Christian political vision is found in the Coronation Order of 973. In that year, King Edgar, now aged thirty, was solemnly crowned at Bath, and received the homage of the British rulers at Chester.

Dunstan deepened the existing hallowed rites by his theological teaching. Most notably, he extracted from the king, prior to the act of crowning, a formal promise that he would respect the liberty and integrity of the church, act consistently against theft and violence, and rule with justice and mercy. Only on that basis could he receive the blessing and anointing of God for his rule. Dunstan thus established the fundamental principle that authority is accountable to God and to his people, in a way that would influence English political development for many centuries.

The coronation itself took place at Pentecost, the feast of the Holy Spirit, whose coming signifies the restoration of unity to mankind in the Church. The king was consecrated, like a bishop, to the service of God and his people, and was hailed as one standing in the long line of anointed Old Testament kings. Each item of the regalia carried a solemn spiritual meaning. The king was to serve as the mediator between God and his people, with the advice of the Church. His rule over the whole British Isles was portrayed as a Christian empire within the providential purposes of God.

On the one hand, this carried forward a long process whereby the Church had been transforming traditional Anglo-Saxon expectations of tribal kingship. On the other hand, Dunstan's action definitely expressed by deeper theology the marriage between Crown and Church, later defined by Wulfstan, Archbishop of York, who said that 'a Christian king was God's representative among a Christian people.'

This concept of authority ran throughout Anglo-Saxon history, and it determined their understanding of the role of abbots and abbesses, bishops and kings. It permeated Bede's *History* and had its origin in the *Pastoral Rule* of St Gregory the Great. He asserted that the distinct nature of Christian leadership and authority could be summed up in the image of Christ as the Servant and Shepherd of God's people, and he declared the ministry of the papacy to be that of 'the servant of the servants of Christ.' Alfred the Great ordered the translation of Gregory's book from Latin into English and circulated it to all his bishops. There is no doubt that the portrait of Dunstan in the first *Life* owes much to this understanding of Christian authority:

> Dunstan could discern with a wise and astute judgement what was true and what was false between people. He could bring agreement and peace by his calming words to the troublesome and quarrelsome. He aided widows and orphans, pilgrims and strangers, in their several needs by his kindly assistance, and would separate unjust marriages by a just deliberation. He strengthened Christian moral values throughout every level of society by his timely advice and his own example. He was fearless in his mode of enquiry, but gentle and trustworthy in the way he supported the interests of others to the benefit of the Church of God. He was completely open to men and women who were quite uneducated, and taught them carefully the wisdom of the Gospel.

Two of the prayers included in Dunstan's Coronation Order sum up well the spirit of his political theology:

> May God the Son of God, our Lord Jesus Christ, who was anointed by His Father with the oil of gladness above His fellows, pour the blessing of the Holy Spirit on your head by the grace of this sacred anointing, and cause it to penetrate your innermost heart. May you prove worthy to reign with Him eternally by virtue of this visible and tangible gift, and so possess each kingdom, temporal and spiritual, on account of your just acts of government.

> O God, you rule your people in love and care for them in virtue: give to this your servant the spirit of wisdom and disciplined rule; that committed to you with all his heart, he may always remain capable to rule in your kingdom. Under your guidance may the security of your Church be upheld

in his time, and may the Christian religion flourish in peace. May he so persevere in good works that, by your guidance, he may attain to your heavenly Kingdom.

The Disciple of Christ

Dunstan's vision of Christ coloured his whole understanding of prayer and authority in church and state, and it is most fully glimpsed in one of the great works of liturgical art associated with his time at Canterbury, the *Sherborne Pontifical*. This is a book containing the blessings and other prayers proper to the office of the archbishop, and it was given to one of Dunstan's pupils, Wulfsige, who, having been Abbot of Westminster, went to serve the see of Sherborne shortly after Dunstan's death. It is characteristic of a family of manuscripts drawn up at Canterbury during Dunstan's primacy and shortly after. Its association with him is almost certain because it contains the personal charge given him by the pope when he went to Rome in 961 to receive the *pallium*, the symbol of his authority as Archbishop of Canterbury.

The book is prefaced by a sequence of four remarkable line drawings, similar to the one of Christ as the Wisdom of God made by Dunstan in the manuscript he edited at Glastonbury. The first is an exquisite picture of the Crucifixion, probably inserted by a later Canterbury artist when the book was prepared as a gift to the new bishop of Sherborne. It is one of many such profoundly contemplative portrayals of Christ, serene in death, affirmed by the hand of God, and supported by angels. St Mary and St John stand on either side rapt in silent contemplation. This type of crucifixion can also be discerned in some of the stone-carved roods, as well as in other manuscripts, that remain from the late Anglo-Saxon period.

But the next sequence of pictures is unique, and they were probably commissioned by Dunstan himself as a visual commentary on the specific theological emphases of the pope's charge that immediately follows them. They reveal the Christology that lay at the heart of all that Dunstan stood for as abbot and archbishop. The first portrays Christ as King, crowned and bearing a book and a rod as in the earlier Glastonbury picture. The second portrays Christ as herald of the gospel, again with a book but also carrying a cross. The last picture is more ethereal and probably portrays the Risen Christ in the garden which speaks of Paradise, bearing the palm of victory in martyrdom and also an unmarked book, perhaps still sealed, with his hand raised in blessing. This three-fold rendition of Christ is without precedent, and reveals Dunstan once again innovating as he used art to express theology and contemplative vision.

The possible lines of interpretation are manifold. There may be a connection with the gifts of the Magi to Christ as King, God and Man. Certainly at Winchester at this time, Christ was being portrayed as a crowned king receiving homage from the Magi, portrayed as three crowned kings. This iconography clearly addressed the Christian transformation of kingship, and it soon spread to Germany and beyond. On the other hand, each figure may represent different aspects of *Christus Victor*, and certainly this emphasis is common in many of the prayers of this period. It is also possible that the three pictures may be connected with the solemn rite of entrance by the archbishop into his cathedral, described at the beginning of the *Pontifical*. Finally, it may be a case of Christology revealing the hidden Trinity of God, Father, Son and Holy Spirit.

Implicit within this sequence of images may also be an understanding of the nature of episcopal primacy entrusted by the pope to Dunstan. The pope inserted into the standard form of a *pallium* charge a direct reference to Christ's teaching about the Good Shepherd in St John 10. These three images may allude to Christ as the shepherd and ruler of the Church;

and to his self-sacrifice in conflict with evil to protect his people; and to his resurrection and his coming again, to hold to account all who share in his pastoral ministry and mission. In the pope's charge all this is indicated, and there is a corresponding movement at the end from Christology to Trinitarian theology, with the implication that pastoral care will lead to contemplative vision, very much in the spirit of St Gregory the Great.

It is interesting that there is also a striking line figure of Christ as the Wisdom of God in a manuscript of St Gregory's *Pastoral Rule* from Christ Church, Canterbury dating from Dunstan's time, and another similar contemporary drawing of Philosophy in a copy of Boethius' *De Consolatione Philosophiae* from St Augustine's monastery at Canterbury.

The Making of a Saint

The first *Life* of St Dunstan is an interesting text because while it contains many ingredients common to hagiography at this time it is not really governed by them. It is in fact highly anecdotal, drawing mainly, it would appear, on the author's own knowledge of Dunstan while they were at Glastonbury, and perhaps just after he moved to Canterbury. It would appear that the writer was a foreigner, based at Liège, but one who had known Dunstan personally. Many of the stories he tells were probably Dunstan's own reminiscences, some of them carrying explanations with reference to passages from the Bible. There are three main strands within the tradition which illuminate Dunstan's personal spiritual formation.

The first is that from an early age Dunstan felt called by God, and various things happened to him that he interpreted as signs of divine favour and protection: for example, his childhood vision at Glastonbury, a miraculous escape when he climbed up onto the church roof there during a fever, and his youthful abilities in the study of theology. Then there were moments when he had to stand against the prevailing attitudes of his peers at court, and met with abuse and contempt at their hands for his spiritual and artistic gifts. On two occasions he was nearly injured by stones apparently falling off churches—one of which might have been a meteorite.

This last pair of events points to the second main strand; a running conflict with evil, which opposed him at every turn in the first part of his life, and especially as he established monastic life and education at Glastonbury. Sometimes this took the form of opposition and intrigue at court. On other occasions it infiltrated his prayers in the form of fierce beasts and fantasies. He engaged evil by prayer and fortitude even when attacks went on day and night relentlessly: 'in these ways the ancient seducer often wearied the blessed father Dunstan as in a mindless conflict.' His appointments both to Glastonbury and later to Canterbury were heralded by sharp political danger and spiritual conflict.

His life of prayer made Dunstan acutely sensitive to manifestations of evil in other contexts, notably at court, and on more than one occasion, through the gift of second sight, he was able to foresee the deaths of kings and of members of his own community at Glastonbury. By prayerful intuition he was able to sense, during his exile abroad, the travails his monks were undergoing.

This faculty developed to the point where Dunstan often sensed and glimpsed the reality of heaven in his prayers, and while asleep: this was the third strand in his spirituality. He saw his spiritual mother Ethelfleda, as she lay dying at Glastonbury, being visited by the Holy Spirit in the form of a white dove full of flashing light and beauty. On another occasion, while designing vestments at a nunnery, he heard his harp play the music of an antiphon: *The souls of the saints rejoice in heaven, who have followed the footsteps of Christ; and who for love of Him have shed their blood: they shall reign with Christ forever.* This is an interesting text because it conjoins martyrdom to the monastic vocation. This was a dominant theme in Anglo-Saxon spirituality, having received its fullest statement in the early eighth century, in Aldhelm's work *On Virginity*, which was widely circulated in the reformed monasteries of the tenth century.

The first biographer tells little of substance about Dunstan's work as Archbishop of Canterbury after 960, but instead continues with spiritual anecdotes, some of which may have come from any period of his life. Of particular interest is the story of Dunstan's vision of his mother in heaven, during which he learned music, which he was able to dictate to one of his monks the next day. Apparently this occurred on several occasions, and there is a form of the *Kyries* that was associated with Dunstan throughout the middle ages—the *Kyrie Rex Splendens.* Dunstan himself was a practising musician and harpist.

Perhaps towards the end of his life comes the lovely story of how he used to go across to the monastery of St Augustine while in Canterbury, to pray during the night. While praying to the Mother of God at the eastern end of the church, he heard sweet and unexpected singing. Peeping through a hole in the screen, he saw the chapel filled with shining light, and a crowd of virgins singing the hymn by Sedulius: *Let us sing, O friends, let us sing to the honour of the Lord: let the sweet love of Christ sound through pious lips.'*

The second *Life* of Dunstan was written for a different purpose: to provide the readings for the monastic office commemorating him at Canterbury Cathedral in the early eleventh century. By this time, the feast of Dunstan was commanded by law to be observed nationally on 19th May, the date of his death. This *Life* summarises, and in places augments, many of the traditions in the first *Life*, but it is very much briefer and less circumstantial. It is most interesting for the account it gives of the manner of his dying.

It asserts that Dunstan was forewarned by angels of his death, but refused to leave until after he had celebrated the feast of the Ascension in his cathedral. So instead he was commanded by the angels to be ready to depart on the Saturday following 'to sing the *Sanctus* before the pope himself in Rome'. Strange words indeed, but Dunstan had of course been to Rome to receive his 'pallium' as archbishop in 961, and perhaps had made an earlier visit as well.

His last sermon left an indelible impression: the people gazed on him 'as if he were an angel of God'. The first biographer also relates in some detail this memorable occasion. He tells how after the service, Dunstan took to his bed, 'with his bald head glistening with light'. One manuscript of the first *Life* also tells how during this waiting period, Dunstan's bed was on occasion elevated from the ground.

It is, however, the second biographer's description of his dying which is the most vivid, and must rest on the personal testimony of someone who was there. Perhaps Alphege, the Archbishop of Canterbury to whom this work is dedicated, was the authority. He was a close friend and protégé of Dunstan, being Bishop of Winchester at the time of Dunstan's death in 988:

> From the day of the Lord's Ascension, this pillar of God began slowly to lose his strength; weariness overcame him and he went to bed for the rest of the week. On Saturday morning, just after the close of the night office, he summoned his community to him. He commended his spirit to their prayers, and received the Eucharist for the last time as it was celebrated in his presence. Then giving thanks to God, he began to sing: 'The gracious and most merciful Lord hath so done his marvellous works that they ought to be held in remembrance; He hath given meat unto them that fear Him.' (Psalm 111. 4-5) With these words on his lips, he rendered his spirit into the hands of his Creator. How happy he whom the Lord found thus watching! He

was buried in a grave of his own making, in the cathedral where he had taught his own people, while as a bishop he passed among them.'

A Life-Giver

The tomb of Dunstan in Canterbury Cathedral soon became a place of pilgrimage and healing. Sometime after the Norman Conquest, a monk of Christ Church, called Osbern, wrote a new *Life* of the saint to persuade Lanfranc, the Norman archbishop, to reinstate Dunstan's cult. He enlisted the sympathetic help of St Anselm, and when he in turn became archbishop he expressed his profound reverence for the saint. What is valuable about Osbern's work is his first-hand account of the miracles of healing and deliverance that occurred at the tomb of Dunstan throughout his own lifetime. He recalls the earliest miracles of healing—of blind people, and former dependents of the saint. Then he describes what he and his fellow schoolboys witnessed in the cathedral, sometimes surreptitiously!

There follows a fascinating account of miracles associated with Dunstan that affected the monastic community during the often stormy period of Lanfranc's early rule. Osbern shows how Lanfranc was obliged in the end no longer to ignore so prominent an English saint. Finally Osbern speaks about some occurrences in his personal life and experience in which he sensed the saint's protection and intervention. The veneration felt by St Anselm for Dunstan is perhaps the most notable, for Anselm was a highly able and discerning person. He had a vision of Dunstan just before his own death.

In the mind of Dunstan's contemporaries he was an outstanding Christian. They describe him as an unshakeable 'pillar of God'. His loving and angelic character is also often remarked upon. At home and abroad, he was regarded as the 'jewel of the English' and a true patron of his country, a faithful priest and bishop, a true friend, and a charismatic teacher and father-in-God.

The abiding spirit of this appreciation is best captured in some of the liturgical material that remains, with which English Christians commemorated his cult. Their love for him grew more poignant as they endured repeated attacks by the Vikings, and in the end, conquest by the Normans:

O eternal God, you enriched blessed Dunstan with many virtues, and endowed him with grace poured upon grace. He was always untiring in his love of you on earth, and so now is able to contemplate unceasingly the vision of your blessedness in heaven. You made him faithful in the care of your Church, and now you have set him over all your good things, filling him with blessing and joy.

We pray that, in your all-powerful mercy, we may be loosed from the bonds of our sins by his merits, and being confirmed in our own holy vocation, we may attain to the glory of your heavenly Kingdom, where each person arriving will hear your words: 'Well done! Good and faithful servant'. We ask this through Jesus Christ our Lord.

O merciful confessor of Christ, O light and teacher of the English people: O Dunstan, the good shepherd and upholder of our whole land! Be the healer of the various ailments of those who visit your tomb. As we now abase ourselves before your holy merits, which stand confirmed before Heaven's high throne; pray to God to deliver our land from its enemies, loose us from the bonds of our sins, and lead us, we pray, to eternal life in the end; through Jesus Christ our Lord.

May God, the Light of the ages, who caused His noble and eminent bishop, Dunstan, to shine forth in our time like one of the apostles, fill you with heavenly blessing on account of his merits; that following the footsteps of so resplendent a predecessor, you may be able to mount the ladder of divine ascent.

May He who foreordained that so venerable, glorious, unique and angelic a patron should arise for the English people, kindle in you a burning desire to reach the place where this magnificent saint ever flourishes among the choirs of angels in Heaven. Amen.

Alleluia! Come, beloved Dunstan, and pray for your humble servants before the throne of Christ in Heaven. Alleluia!

Further Reading

Called to be Angels: An Introduction to Anglo-Saxon Spirituality, D. J. Dales (Canterbury Press, 1998)

The Monastic Order in England, 940-1216, D. Knowles, (Cambridge University Press, 2nd edition, 1966)

Dunstan, Saint and Statesman, D. J. Dales (Lutterworth Press, Cambridge, 1988)

St Dunstan, his Life, Times & Cult, ed. N. Ramsay, M. Sparks and T. Tatton-Brown, (Boydell Press, Ipswich, 1992)

Christ the Golden Blossom: a Treasury of Anglo-Saxon Prayer, ed. D. J. Dales, (Canterbury Press, 2000)

Regularis Concordia, ed. T. Symons, (London, 1953)